How to Stop Being Defensive

A Guide to unleash your Authentic self
and Overcoming Defensiveness

By Sarah Moore

Table of contents

In a world filled with constant challenges and interactions, it's only natural to find ourselves grappling with defensiveness. We often shield ourselves, constructing protective walls that hinder our growth and limit the depth of our relationships. But what if we could break free from this self-imposed barrier? What if we could discover the power within us to embrace vulnerability, open ourselves to growth, and live authentically?

Welcome to "How to Stop Being Defensive: A Guide to Unleash Your Authentic Self and Overcome Defensiveness." In this book, we embark on a transformative journey to explore the intricate layers of defensiveness and discover the keys to unlocking our true selves.

Defensiveness is a common human trait that emerges as a response to perceived threats or criticisms. It acts as a shield, protecting us from discomfort and shielding us from potential harm. However, this self-defense mechanism often comes at a cost. It prevents us from truly connecting with others, inhibits personal growth, and hampers our ability to navigate life's challenges with resilience.

This guidebook is designed to empower you with valuable insights, practical tools, and transformative exercises that will help you break free from the shackles of defensiveness. By exploring the root causes and underlying emotions that fuel defensiveness, we will embark on a journey of self-discovery and self-acceptance.

Throughout these pages, you will learn to recognize the patterns of defensiveness in your own life and understand how they impact your relationships, personal growth, and overall well-being. You will discover techniques to develop emotional intelligence, strengthen your communication skills, and foster genuine connections based on trust and understanding.

Furthermore, this book goes beyond theory and provides you with actionable strategies to implement in your daily life. From mindfulness practices and self-reflection exercises to practical tips for embracing vulnerability and managing conflict, you will gain a comprehensive toolkit to navigate defensiveness and foster personal growth.

Remember, the journey toward overcoming defensiveness is not a solitary one. By engaging with the insights and stories shared within these pages, you will realize that you are not alone. This book serves as a guide, offering support and encouragement as you embark on a path towards self-discovery and transformation.

It's time to shed the armor that keeps you from experiencing life to its fullest. It's time to reclaim your authenticity, strengthen your relationships, and embrace the beauty of vulnerability. Are you ready to embark on this transformative journey? Let us begin our exploration of how to stop being defensive and unleash your authentic self.

Welcome to a life of growth, connection, and true liberation.

Chapter 1

Understanding Defensiveness - The Hidden Barrier

Defensiveness is a common human reaction that arises when we perceive a threat to our self-image or beliefs. It acts as a protective mechanism, aiming to shield us from emotional pain, criticism, or vulnerability. While defensiveness may serve a temporary purpose, it often hampers personal growth and strains relationships. Therefore, it is crucial to understand its dynamics, recognize its detrimental effects, and develop self-awareness as the initial step towards change.

Section 2: The Psychology of Defensiveness
The Nature of Defensiveness
Defensiveness is deeply rooted in our psychological makeup and can manifest in various ways. It often arises when our core values, beliefs, or actions are challenged, causing a defensive response to protect our ego. This

response can range from denying, justifying, or deflecting criticism to outright hostility or withdrawal.

Triggers and Threats to Self-Image
Defensiveness is typically triggered by perceived threats to our self-image. These threats can come in the form of criticism, disagreement, or even minor setbacks that challenge our competence, intelligence, or integrity. The more attached we are to our self-image, the stronger the defensive reaction may be.

2.3 The Role of Fear and Insecurity
Fear and insecurity play a significant role in fueling defensiveness. The fear of being judged, rejected, or exposed as inadequate can provoke a defensive response. Insecurity about our abilities or fear of losing control may also contribute to defensiveness as a way to maintain a sense of stability and security.

Section 3: Detrimental Effects on Personal Growth
Hindering Feedback and Learning
Defensiveness can impede personal growth by inhibiting our ability to accept feedback and learn from

our mistakes. When we are defensive, we are less receptive to constructive criticism and miss valuable opportunities for self-improvement.

Strained Relationships
Defensiveness can strain relationships by creating barriers to effective communication and understanding. When we become defensive during conflicts or disagreements, it becomes difficult to have open and honest conversations. This can lead to misunderstandings, resentment, and a breakdown in trust.

Stagnation and Resistance to Change
Defensiveness can result in stagnation and resistance to change. By protecting our self-image, we may resist exploring new ideas, perspectives, or experiences that could facilitate personal growth. This resistance limits our potential for self-discovery and adaptation.

Section 4: Cultivating Self-Awareness as the First Step Towards Change
Recognizing Defensiveness Patterns

Developing self-awareness involves recognizing our defensive patterns and understanding the underlying emotions and beliefs that drive them. By paying attention to our thoughts, reactions, and behaviors during triggering situations, we can identify when defensiveness arises.

Exploring Root Causes
Self-awareness also involves exploring the root causes of defensiveness. This may include examining past experiences, childhood upbringing, and core beliefs that contribute to our defensive tendencies. Understanding these underlying factors can provide valuable insights into our defensive behaviors.

Practicing Mindfulness and Reflection
Mindfulness and reflection techniques can help cultivate self-awareness and reduce defensiveness. By practicing being present in the moment, observing our thoughts and emotions without judgment, we can gain clarity and distance ourselves from automatic defensive reactions.

Seeking Support and Feedback

Seeking support from trusted individuals or professionals can aid in developing self-awareness. Honest feedback from others can provide valuable perspectives on our defensive tendencies, helping us gain new insights and challenge ingrained defensive patterns.

Section 5: Strategies for Overcoming Defensiveness

5.1 Embracing Vulnerability

Overcoming defensiveness requires embracing vulnerability. Recognizing that vulnerability is not a weakness but a strength can help us let go of the need to defend ourselves constantly. Opening up to others and expressing our true feelings and thoughts can foster deeper connections and facilitate personal growth.

Active Listening and Empathy

Active listening and empathy are powerful antidotes to defensiveness. When engaged in a conversation, focus on understanding the other person's perspective rather than immediately reacting defensively. Practice empathy by putting yourself in their shoes, seeking to understand their emotions and experiences.

Reframing Criticism as an Opportunity
Instead of perceiving criticism as a personal attack, reframe it as an opportunity for growth. Recognize that feedback can provide valuable insights and constructive guidance for self-improvement. Approach criticism with an open mind, seeking to understand and learn from it rather than becoming defensive.

5.4 Practicing Emotional Regulation
Developing emotional regulation skills can help manage defensiveness. When faced with triggering situations, take a pause, and engage in calming techniques such as deep breathing or mindfulness exercises. This allows you to respond thoughtfully rather than react defensively in the heat of the moment.

Challenging Assumptions and Beliefs
Questioning and challenging our assumptions and beliefs can help reduce defensiveness. Recognize that not all criticism or differing opinions are a direct attack

on your identity. By staying open to alternative perspectives and considering different viewpoints, you can expand your understanding and overcome defensiveness.

Reflecting on Personal Triggers

Reflecting on your personal triggers can provide valuable insights into your defensive reactions. Identify specific situations, topics, or types of feedback that tend to evoke defensiveness in you. Understanding your triggers allows you to anticipate and prepare for them, enabling you to respond more effectively.

Section 6: Conclusion

In this chapter, we explored the psychology behind defensiveness and its detrimental effects on personal growth and relationships. We discussed the importance of cultivating self-awareness as the first step towards change, including recognizing defensiveness patterns, exploring root causes, and practicing mindfulness. Additionally, we provided strategies for overcoming defensiveness, such as embracing vulnerability, active listening, reframing criticism, practicing emotional regulation, challenging beliefs, and reflecting on personal triggers. By developing self-awareness and adopting these strategies, we can break through the hidden barrier of defensiveness and foster personal growth and healthier relationships. In the next chapter, we will explore effective communication techniques to enhance our ability to express ourselves and engage in constructive dialogue.

Chapter 2

The Roots of Defensiveness - Exploring Personal Triggers

Defensiveness is a common emotional response that can arise in various situations. When we feel attacked, criticized, or challenged, our instinctive reaction may be to protect ourselves and guard our beliefs, actions, or self-image. However, defensiveness often stems from deeper emotional roots that are worth exploring. By delving into our emotional history and childhood experiences, identifying recurring patterns and triggers, and unearthing unresolved emotions, we can gain valuable insights into our defensive reactions and work towards more constructive and authentic responses.

Digging Deep into Your Emotional History and Childhood Experiences:

To understand the roots of defensiveness, it is essential to embark on a journey of self-reflection and introspection. Our emotional history and childhood experiences play a significant role in shaping our beliefs, behaviors, and responses as adults. Early life experiences, such as inconsistent parenting, excessive criticism, traumatic events, or the absence of emotional validation, can contribute to the development of defense mechanisms as coping strategies.

Exploring these experiences requires a willingness to confront and examine past wounds and their impact on our present reactions. Engaging in therapy, journaling, or talking with a trusted confidant can provide a safe space for this exploration, helping us uncover the underlying factors that contribute to our defensiveness.

Identifying Recurring Patterns and Triggers:

Defensiveness often manifests as a reaction to specific triggers or situations. These triggers can vary from person to person, but they typically involve perceived threats to our self-worth, autonomy, or beliefs. By observing and identifying these recurring patterns and triggers, we can gain valuable insights into our defensive reactions.

It can be helpful to ask ourselves questions such as: What situations or topics consistently provoke defensiveness in me? Are there any commonalities among these triggers? Do they relate to certain aspects of my identity, vulnerabilities, or insecurities? Recognizing these triggers allows us to approach them with increased self-awareness and emotional regulation, paving the way for more constructive responses.

Unearthing Unresolved Emotions and Their Impact:

Defensiveness often masks deeper emotions that have not been fully processed or resolved. Beneath the surface of defensiveness, there may be fear, shame, guilt, anger, or hurt waiting to be acknowledged and addressed. Unresolved emotions from past experiences can intensify our defensive reactions, as we subconsciously protect ourselves from re-experiencing pain or vulnerability.

By engaging in emotional excavation, we can begin to understand the impact of these unresolved emotions on our defensive tendencies. It may involve revisiting past traumas, exploring our core beliefs and values, and learning to embrace vulnerability. With support from a therapist, counselor, or support group, we can create a safe environment to navigate these emotions, gradually unraveling their grip on our defensive responses.

Moving Towards Constructive Responses:

Once we have gained awareness of our emotional history, identified triggers, and acknowledged unresolved emotions, we can begin to cultivate more constructive responses to perceived threats or challenges.

Developing self-compassion and self-acceptance is crucial in this process. By understanding that defensiveness is often a protective mechanism born out of past pain, we can approach ourselves with kindness and empathy. Practicing active listening, seeking clarification instead of assuming intentions, and engaging in open-minded dialogue can help us reframe our defensiveness as an opportunity for growth and connection.

Additionally, cultivating emotional resilience through self-care practices, such as mindfulness, meditation, and stress reduction techniques, can enhance our ability to respond calmly and authentically in triggering situations.

Conclusion:

Understanding the roots of defensiveness requires a deep dive into our emotional history, childhood experiences, recurring patterns, and triggers. By unearthing unresolved emotions and their impact

Chapter 3

Embracing Vulnerability - The Power of Authenticity

Strength is often glorified along ,self-assuredness, and invulnerability, embracing vulnerability can seem counterintuitive. However, the concept of vulnerability is not synonymous with weakness. Rather, it is an inherent part of our human experience that can lead to profound personal growth, deeper connections with others, and an enhanced sense of authenticity. By challenging societal norms and cultural conditioning that perpetuate defensiveness, we can cultivate self-acceptance and self-compassion, allowing vulnerability to become a powerful tool for personal and interpersonal transformation.

Understanding Vulnerability:

Vulnerability can be defined as the state of being open, exposed, or susceptible to emotional or physical harm. It involves stepping outside our comfort zones and taking emotional risks by allowing ourselves to be seen, heard, and understood. Contrary to popular belief, vulnerability does not signify weakness; rather, it showcases courage, strength, and authenticity.

Overcoming Societal and Cultural Conditioning:

From an early age, we are often conditioned to view vulnerability as a liability. Society teaches us to hide our weaknesses, fears, and insecurities, promoting a culture of defensiveness and emotional detachment. We learn to wear masks to protect ourselves from judgment, criticism, and rejection. However, by challenging these societal norms, we can break free from the shackles of fear and experience the transformative power of vulnerability.

Cultivating Self-Acceptance and Self-Compassion:

One of the key prerequisites for embracing vulnerability is developing self-acceptance and self-compassion. It requires acknowledging and embracing our imperfections, recognizing that vulnerability is an inherent part of the human experience. By practicing self-acceptance, we can release the need for perfection and self-judgment, allowing ourselves to be authentically seen.

When we cultivate self-compassion, we become more understanding and kind toward ourselves. We recognize that vulnerability opens us up to the possibility of failure, disappointment, and rejection, but we learn to treat ourselves with warmth and understanding, just as we would treat a dear friend. Self-compassion creates a safe space within ourselves to explore our vulnerabilities without self-criticism or judgment.

The Power of Authenticity:

Authenticity, often synonymous with vulnerability, is the ability to express oneself genuinely and honestly. When we embrace vulnerability, we remove the mask of pretense and create a space where we can be true to ourselves. This authenticity allows us to form deeper connections with others, as they can sense our sincerity and relate to our shared human experiences.

Authenticity also fosters trust in our relationships. By opening up about our vulnerabilities, we give others the permission to do the same. It creates an environment of empathy, compassion, and understanding, where meaningful connections can flourish. Authenticity builds bridges between individuals and dismantles barriers, allowing us to build more genuine and fulfilling relationships.

Personal and Interpersonal Transformation:

Embracing vulnerability leads to personal growth and transformation. When we allow ourselves to be vulnerable, we confront our fears and step outside our comfort zones. This process expands our emotional resilience, enhances our self-awareness, and deepens our understanding of ourselves and others.

Through vulnerability, we can also inspire and empower those around us. By embracing our authentic selves, we give others the courage to do the same. Our vulnerability becomes a source of strength, encouraging others to open up, express their emotions, and embrace their own vulnerabilities.

Embracing vulnerability is a powerful act of self-love and authenticity. It allows us to break free from the limitations of societal conditioning, cultivate self-acceptance and self-compassion, and foster deeper connections with others. By embracing vulnerability, we embark on a journey of personal and interpersonal transformation empowers us to live more fulfilling and meaningful lives.

However, it is important to note that embracing vulnerability does not mean recklessness or exposing ourselves to unnecessary harm. It is about consciously choosing to be open and authentic while setting healthy boundaries and practicing self-care. It is a delicate balance between being vulnerable and ensuring our emotional well-being.

To further embrace vulnerability, it can be helpful to practice the following:

Cultivate emotional awareness: Developing a deep understanding of our emotions allows us to recognize when we are closing off or avoiding vulnerability. By acknowledging and accepting our emotions, we can better navigate them and respond authentically.

Practice active listening: Being present and fully engaged in conversations with others creates a safe space for vulnerability. By genuinely listening to others without judgment or interruption, we encourage open and honest communication.

Seek support: Surrounding ourselves with supportive and trustworthy individuals creates a supportive network where vulnerability is welcomed. Sharing our thoughts, fears, and challenges with empathetic friends, family, or therapists can provide comfort and encouragement on our journey.

Embrace failure and learn from it: Vulnerability often involves taking risks, and sometimes those risks may result in failure. Embracing failure as an opportunity for growth and learning helps us develop resilience and adaptability. It allows us to view setbacks as stepping stones toward personal development.

Practice self-reflection: Taking time for introspection and self-reflection enables us to gain insights into our values, desires, and fears. Journaling, meditation, or engaging in activities that promote self-awareness can deepen our understanding of ourselves and facilitate vulnerability.

Celebrate authenticity: Recognize and celebrate the moments when you allow yourself to be vulnerable and authentic. Acknowledge the courage it takes to be true to yourself and appreciate the positive impact it has on your well-being and relationships.

In conclusion, embracing vulnerability is a powerful act that transforms our lives. It requires challenging societal conditioning, cultivating self-acceptance and self-compassion, and fostering authentic connections with others. By stepping into vulnerability, we unlock personal growth, deeper relationships, and a profound sense of authenticity. It is through embracing our vulnerabilities that we truly discover the strength within us and experience the power of authenticity.

Chapter 4

Active Listening - The Art of Connection

Active listening is indeed a crucial skill when it comes to fostering healthy dialogue and creating meaningful connections with others. By actively listening, we demonstrate our genuine interest in understanding others, which helps to build trust and dismantle defensiveness in communication. Here's how active listening contributes to these goals:

Dismantling defensiveness: When people feel heard and understood, they are more likely to let their guard down and engage in open and honest communication. Active listening involves giving your full attention to the speaker, showing empathy, and refraining from judgment or interruption. By doing so, you create an environment where defensiveness is less likely to arise, and individuals feel more comfortable expressing themselves.

Effective communication skills: Active listening goes beyond simply hearing the words being spoken. It involves paying attention to the speaker's tone, body language, and emotions to fully understand their message. This comprehensive understanding allows you to respond more effectively, demonstrating empathy and validating their experiences. By practicing active listening, you can improve your communication skills and establish a stronger connection with others.

Creating a safe space: When engaging in dialogue, it's crucial to create a safe space where individuals feel free to express themselves without fear of judgment. Active listening plays a significant role in this process. By giving your undivided attention, maintaining an open mind, and providing nonverbal cues like nodding or maintaining eye contact, you communicate your willingness to listen without judgment. This encourages others to share their thoughts, emotions, and experiences more openly, fostering a safe and supportive environment.

In summary, active listening is an essential component of effective communication. By actively engaging with others, practicing empathy, and creating a nonjudgmental space, you can foster healthy dialogue, build stronger connections, and dismantle defensiveness, ultimately promoting understanding and meaningful relationships.

Here are a few additional points on the importance of active listening in fostering connections and effective communication:

Enhancing understanding: Active listening allows you to gain a deeper understanding of the speaker's perspective, emotions, and needs. By fully immersing yourself in the conversation and actively seeking to comprehend their point of view, you can avoid making assumptions or jumping to conclusions. This understanding forms the foundation for meaningful connections and paves the way for effective problem-solving and collaboration.

Building trust and rapport: Active listening demonstrates your genuine interest and respect for the speaker. By giving them your full attention, you convey that their thoughts and feelings are valued. This builds trust and rapport over time, as people are more likely to engage in open and honest conversations when they feel acknowledged and respected. Trust is a fundamental element of any healthy relationship, and active listening helps to cultivate it.

Conflict resolution: Active listening is a powerful tool for resolving conflicts and disagreements. By listening attentively, you allow each party to express their grievances, concerns, and perspectives. This not only helps them feel heard and understood but also provides an opportunity for finding common ground and mutually acceptable solutions. Active listening helps to de-escalate conflicts, promote empathy, and foster a collaborative approach to resolving differences.

Strengthening relationships: When you actively listen to others, you demonstrate that their thoughts and feelings matter to you. This strengthens your relationships by fostering a sense of validation, empathy, and support. Active listening enables you to connect with others on a deeper level, enhancing the quality of your interactions and creating a sense of emotional intimacy.

Personal growth and learning: Active listening is not only beneficial for the speaker but also for the listener. By opening yourself up to different perspectives and experiences, you broaden your understanding of the world. Active listening allows you to learn from others, expand your knowledge, challenge your own assumptions, and develop a more inclusive mindset.

In conclusion, active listening is a transformative skill that promotes understanding, trust, and healthy dialogue. By actively engaging with others, you can foster connections, resolve conflicts, and create a supportive environment where everyone feels heard and valued. It is a lifelong practice that enhances both personal growth and the quality of our relationships.

Chapter 5

Responding, Not Reacting - Navigating Difficult Situations

In life, we often find ourselves facing challenging and difficult situations that test our patience, resilience, and emotional intelligence. How we navigate these moments can greatly impact the outcomes and relationships involved. It is crucial to learn the art of responding, not reacting, as this approach allows us to unravel automatic reactions and replace them with thoughtful responses. By managing conflict with grace and empathy, and developing emotional intelligence to defuse tense situations, we can effectively navigate difficult scenarios and maintain positive connections with others.

Unraveling Automatic Reactions

Human beings are wired to react quickly to stimuli, especially when we feel threatened or provoked. These automatic reactions are often fueled by our emotions and can lead to impulsive behavior and poor decision-making. However, it is essential to recognize that we have the power to unravel these automatic reactions and choose a more deliberate response.

The first step in unraveling automatic reactions is self-awareness. By being mindful of our thoughts, emotions, and bodily sensations in challenging situations, we can gain insight into our automatic responses. Taking a pause, both mentally and physically, allows us to create a space between the trigger and our reaction. This pause enables us to assess the situation more objectively and make a conscious decision about how we want to respond.

Once we have established this awareness and pause, we can explore alternative perspectives and consider the consequences of different responses. By questioning our initial reactions and examining the underlying assumptions and beliefs, we open ourselves up to more constructive possibilities. This process of unraveling automatic reactions requires practice and self-reflection, but over time, it can become a valuable habit that promotes better communication and problem-solving.

Managing Conflict with Grace and Empathy

Conflict is an inevitable part of life, and how we handle it can significantly impact our relationships and overall well-being. When faced with difficult situations or conflicts, responding with grace and empathy can help foster understanding, promote cooperation, and prevent further escalation.

To manage conflict with grace, it is essential to approach the situation with an open mind and a willingness to listen. Active listening involves giving the other person your full attention, suspending judgment, and seeking to understand their perspective. By demonstrating empathy and validating their feelings and concerns, you create a safe space for open dialogue and collaboration.

In addition to listening and empathy, effective communication skills play a vital role in managing conflict gracefully. Clearly expressing your thoughts and feelings using "I" statements can help avoid blame and defensiveness. It is important to focus on the issue at hand rather than attacking the person, and to be mindful of non-verbal cues such as body language and tone of voice.

Collaborative problem-solving is another key aspect of managing conflict with grace. By working together to find mutually beneficial solutions, you can build trust and strengthen relationships. This requires a willingness to compromise, explore different options, and find common ground.

Developing Emotional Intelligence to Defuse Tense Situations

Emotional intelligence, often referred to as EQ, is the ability to recognize and manage one's own emotions and effectively understand and respond to the emotions of others. Developing emotional intelligence is crucial when navigating difficult situations, as it allows us to defuse tense moments, build rapport, and find constructive resolutions.

Self-awareness is the foundation of emotional intelligence. By understanding our own emotions, triggers, and patterns of behavior, we can better regulate our responses in challenging situations. This self-awareness enables us to pause and choose a response that aligns with our values and long-term goals, rather than succumbing to impulsive reactions driven by anger or frustration.

Empathy is another vital component of emotional intelligence. By putting ourselves in the shoes of others and seeking to understand their emotions and perspectives, we can cultivate compassion and create an environment of understanding and respect.

In diffusing tense situations, it is important to practice emotional regulation. This involves managing our own emotions and reactions in a way that does not escalate the conflict further. Taking deep breaths, practicing mindfulness, or using relaxation techniques can help calm our nervous system and prevent us from becoming overwhelmed by intense emotions.

Active listening is a valuable skill when it comes to diffusing tense situations. By giving our full attention to the other person, we demonstrate respect and a genuine interest in understanding their point of view. Avoid interrupting or formulating responses while the other person is speaking, and instead focus on truly hearing and comprehending their words.

Non-verbal communication also plays a significant role in diffusing tension. Our body language, facial expressions, and tone of voice can either escalate or de-escalate a situation. Maintaining an open posture, making eye contact, and using a calm and respectful tone can help create a more positive and conducive atmosphere for resolving conflicts.

In some cases, it may be necessary to take a break from the situation to allow emotions to settle and for both parties to regain composure. This can be particularly useful when emotions are running high and rational discussion becomes challenging. Agreeing to reconvene at a later time, when everyone is calmer and more open to finding a resolution, can prevent further damage to the relationship.

Developing emotional intelligence also involves practicing empathy and understanding the perspectives and emotions of others. Recognizing that everyone has their own unique experiences, values, and beliefs can help cultivate empathy and foster a more compassionate approach to difficult situations. By acknowledging and validating the emotions of others, we create an environment that encourages open communication and collaboration.

Furthermore, it is important to remember that difficult situations and conflicts can provide opportunities for growth and learning. By approaching these situations with a growth mindset, we can view them as chances to develop our emotional intelligence, enhance our communication skills, and strengthen our relationships. Each challenging encounter can serve as a stepping stone towards becoming more adept at responding thoughtfully and effectively in the face of difficulty.

In conclusion, responding, not reacting, is a skill that can greatly benefit us in navigating difficult situations. By unraveling automatic reactions, managing conflict with grace and empathy, and developing emotional intelligence, we can approach challenging scenarios with a calm and thoughtful mindset. These strategies not only contribute to more positive outcomes but also help to build stronger relationships, foster understanding, and promote personal growth.

Chapter 6

Self-Reflection and Personal Growth: Unveiling the Path to Self-Discovery

In the quest for personal growth and self-improvement, there is a powerful tool that often goes unnoticed: self-reflection. The art of self-reflection allows individuals to delve into their innermost thoughts, emotions, and experiences, ultimately leading to a deeper understanding of oneself. By engaging in this process, individuals can uncover hidden truths, identify areas for improvement, and embark on a transformative journey towards personal growth.

Self-reflection acts as a mirror that reflects our thoughts, beliefs, and behaviors. It provides a unique opportunity to examine our choices, actions, and motivations, and to gain insights into the impact they have on our lives and the lives of others. Through self-reflection, we can identify patterns and recurring themes that shape our experiences, both positive and negative. By understanding these patterns, we become better equipped to make conscious decisions and take intentional actions aligned with our values and aspirations.

A crucial aspect of self-reflection is the practice of self-compassion and forgiveness. When we reflect on our past actions or mistakes, it is essential to approach ourselves with kindness and understanding. Acknowledging our imperfections and accepting them as part of our human nature allows us to let go of self-judgment and embrace growth with an open heart. By cultivating self-compassion, we create a nurturing environment for personal development, enabling us to learn from our past and move forward with renewed purpose.

Forgiveness is another powerful catalyst for personal growth that often arises during self-reflection. Holding onto past resentments or grievances weighs us down and hinders our progress. Through self-reflection, we can explore and understand the underlying causes of our hurts and grievances, ultimately allowing us to forgive ourselves and others. By releasing the emotional baggage that burdens us, we open ourselves up to new opportunities and experiences, paving the way for personal growth and fulfillment.

To harness the full potential of self-reflection, it is crucial to set realistic goals and embrace the concept of continuous improvement. Setting goals that are specific, measurable, achievable, relevant, and time-bound (SMART goals) provides a framework for personal growth. These goals act as guiding lights, directing our efforts towards specific areas of improvement. However, it is important to strike a balance between setting ambitious goals and being realistic about our capabilities. Overwhelming ourselves with unattainable objectives can lead to frustration and hinder our progress. Instead, setting incremental goals allows for steady growth and builds momentum as we achieve each milestone.

Embracing continuous improvement is a mindset that encourages us to embrace the journey of personal growth rather than fixating on the end result. It involves a commitment to lifelong learning and a willingness to adapt and evolve. Through self-reflection, we can assess our progress, identify areas for improvement, and make adjustments along the way. This iterative process of reflection, action, and refinement enables us to navigate the ever-changing landscape of personal growth and continuously strive for our best selves.

In conclusion, self-reflection is a powerful tool for personal growth and self-discovery. By engaging in this practice, we can uncover deeper truths about ourselves, cultivate self-compassion and forgiveness, set realistic goals, and embrace continuous improvement. As we embark on this transformative journey, let us remember that personal growth is not a destination but a lifelong process. Through self-reflection, we unlock our potential and become active participants in shaping our own lives, leading to a more fulfilling and purposeful existence.

Here's an extended section on the benefits of self-reflection and personal growth:

Benefits of Self-Reflection and Personal Growth

Self-reflection and personal growth offer numerous benefits that extend beyond individual development. By dedicating time and effort to introspection and self-improvement, individuals can experience positive changes in various aspects of their lives.

Enhanced Self-Awareness: Self-reflection allows individuals to gain a deeper understanding of their thoughts, emotions, strengths, and weaknesses. By becoming more self-aware, individuals can make informed decisions, align their actions with their values, and improve their relationships with others. Self-awareness also fosters empathy and understanding, as individuals gain insights into their own experiences, making it easier to relate to the experiences of others.

Improved Emotional Intelligence: Engaging in self-reflection enhances emotional intelligence, which is the ability to understand and manage emotions effectively. By reflecting on past experiences and emotional reactions, individuals can identify triggers, patterns, and coping mechanisms. This heightened emotional intelligence enables individuals to navigate challenging situations with greater composure, empathy, and resilience.

Clarity of Goals and Priorities: Through self-reflection, individuals can gain clarity on their aspirations, values, and purpose. By understanding their core desires and beliefs, individuals can set meaningful goals and make decisions that are aligned with their authentic selves. This clarity of purpose provides a sense of direction and fulfillment, guiding individuals towards a more purposeful and meaningful life.

Improved Problem-Solving Skills: Self-reflection nurtures critical thinking and problem-solving skills. As individuals engage in introspection, they can analyze their actions, identify areas for improvement, and develop strategies to overcome challenges. This reflective practice enhances creativity, flexibility, and adaptability, empowering individuals to find innovative solutions to problems and make informed decisions.

Strengthened Resilience: Personal growth through self-reflection cultivates resilience, the ability to bounce back from setbacks and adversity. By reflecting on past experiences and lessons learned, individuals develop a resilient mindset that allows them to view failures as opportunities for growth. This resilience enables individuals to navigate obstacles with greater determination, perseverance, and optimism.

Improved Relationships: Self-reflection plays a vital role in nurturing healthy and fulfilling relationships. By understanding ourselves better, we can recognize and manage our emotions, communicate effectively, and empathize with others. This enhanced self-awareness and emotional intelligence lay the foundation for stronger connections, deeper empathy, and more meaningful interactions with loved ones, colleagues, and friends.

Increased Self-Confidence: Engaging in self-reflection and personal growth fosters self-confidence. As individuals recognize their strengths, acknowledge their growth, and embrace self-compassion, they develop a sense of self-assurance. This confidence enables individuals to step out of their comfort zones, pursue new opportunities, and overcome self-doubt, ultimately unlocking their full potential.

Overall Well-being and Happiness: Self-reflection and personal growth contribute significantly to overall well-being and happiness. By actively seeking personal development and aligning their lives with their authentic selves, individuals experience a greater sense of fulfillment and satisfaction. They are more likely to engage in activities that bring them joy, create meaningful relationships, and live a life that is congruent with their values and aspirations.

Incorporating self-reflection into daily life and embracing personal growth is a lifelong journey. It requires dedication, self-compassion, and a willingness to embrace change. However, the rewards are immense, as individuals who engage in self-reflection are more likely to lead fulfilling lives, build meaningful connections, and make positive contributions to the world around them. So, let us embark on this transformative journey of self-discovery, growth, and personal development, unlocking our true potential and living life to the fullest.

Chapter 7

Building Trust and Connection

Building trust through vulnerability and open communication:

One of the most effective ways to build trust in a relationship is through vulnerability and open communication. When you are vulnerable, you allow yourself to be seen and known by others, which creates a deeper sense of connection. Sharing your thoughts, feelings, and fears with someone you trust can help foster intimacy and understanding.

To build trust through vulnerability and open communication, consider the following steps:

Create a safe space: Establish an environment where both parties feel comfortable sharing their thoughts and emotions without fear of judgment or criticism. This requires mutual respect and active listening.

Be authentic: Share your true thoughts and feelings, even if they make you feel exposed or vulnerable. Authenticity promotes trust and encourages the other person to reciprocate by opening up as well.

Practice active listening: When the other person shares their thoughts or feelings, listen attentively and without interruption. Show genuine interest and empathy, and reflect back what you've heard to ensure understanding.

Encourage open dialogue: Encourage the other person to express themselves openly and honestly. Ask open-ended questions that invite deeper conversations and avoid making assumptions or jumping to conclusions.

Respond with empathy: When the other person shares something vulnerable, respond with empathy and understanding. Validate their feelings and experiences, even if you may not fully relate to them. This creates a safe and supportive space for emotional expression.

Nurturing healthy relationships through empathy and understanding:

Empathy and understanding are vital in nurturing healthy relationships. They allow individuals to connect on a deeper level, foster compassion, and promote mutual support. Here are some ways to cultivate empathy and understanding:

Put yourself in the other person's shoes: Try to see things from their perspective and understand their emotions, needs, and concerns. This helps build empathy and prevents judgment or misunderstanding.

Listen actively: Give your full attention when the other person is speaking. Listen not only to their words but also to their tone of voice, body language, and emotions. This helps you grasp their true feelings and experiences.

Validate their emotions: Acknowledge and validate the other person's emotions, even if you don't necessarily agree with them. Show understanding and support rather than dismissing or trivializing their feelings.

Communicate openly and honestly: Share your own thoughts and feelings openly, as this can encourage the other person to do the same. Honest communication fosters understanding and helps bridge gaps in perception or experience.

Practice forgiveness and compassion: Be willing to forgive and let go of past hurts or misunderstandings. Cultivate compassion for yourself and others, recognizing that everyone makes mistakes and has their own struggles.

Healing past wounds and fostering deep connections: Healing past wounds is crucial for fostering deep connections in relationships. Unresolved emotional baggage can create barriers and prevent genuine intimacy. Here are some steps to heal past wounds and foster deeper connections:

Acknowledge and accept the past: Recognize the impact of past wounds and traumas on your current relationships. Acceptance is the first step toward healing.

Seek support: Consider seeking professional help, such as therapy or counseling, to guide you through the healing process. A trained therapist can provide valuable tools and strategies tailored to your specific needs.

Practice self-reflection: Reflect on your own patterns and behaviors in relationships. Identify any negative cycles or unresolved emotions that may be hindering your ability to connect deeply with others.

Communicate your needs: Express your needs and boundaries to those you trust. Clear communication helps create a safe space for healing and fosters understanding between you and others.

Give and receive forgiveness: Forgiveness is a powerful tool for healing. Forgive yourself and others for past mistakes or hurts, allowing room for growth and renewed connections.

Cultivate self-care and self-compassion: Prioritize your own well-being and practice self-care regularly. Nurture yourself physically, emotionally, and mentally. Treat yourself with kindness and compassion, understanding that healing takes time and patience.

Practice active empathy: Put yourself in the shoes of others and actively seek to understand their experiences, perspectives, and emotions. Show empathy and compassion in your interactions, validating their feelings and offering support when needed.

Foster open and honest communication: Create an environment of open and honest communication where all parties feel safe to express their thoughts, concerns, and emotions. Encourage dialogue, active listening, and respect for differing opinions.

Engage in shared experiences: Foster deep connections by engaging in shared activities or experiences. This can be anything from going on adventures together to engaging in meaningful conversations or pursuing common interests. Shared experiences create lasting memories and strengthen the bond between individuals.

Practice patience and understanding: Recognize that healing and deepening connections takes time. Be patient with yourself and others as you navigate the process. Understand that everyone has their own pace and journey, and be supportive along the way.

Celebrate growth and progress: Acknowledge and celebrate the growth and progress made in your relationships. Recognize the efforts put into building trust, nurturing empathy, and healing past wounds. Celebrating milestones and achievements reinforces the positive aspects of your connections.

Remember, building trust, nurturing empathy, and healing past wounds are ongoing processes in relationships. It requires consistent effort, open-mindedness, and a willingness to grow together.

By prioritizing these aspects, you can create stronger, healthier, and more fulfilling connections with others.

Chapter 8

Releasing defensiveness and cultivating inner peace

Releasing defensiveness and cultivating inner peace involve letting go of the need for constant validation and approval from others. Here are some steps you can take to cultivate inner peace and release defensiveness in relation to seeking validation:

Recognize your inherent worth: Understand that your worth as a person is not dependent on external validation or approval. You are valuable and deserving of love and respect simply by being who you are.

Embrace self-acceptance: Practice self-acceptance by acknowledging your strengths, weaknesses, and imperfections. Embracing yourself fully, including your flaws, allows you to develop a stronger sense of self-worth that is not reliant on others' opinions.

Understand the nature of validation: Reflect on the fact that seeking validation from others is a normal human desire but can be fleeting and inconsistent. Recognize that relying solely on external validation puts your peace and happiness in the hands of others, which can be unstable and unsatisfying in the long run.

Develop self-awareness: Cultivate self-awareness by observing your thoughts and emotions when you feel the need for validation arise. Notice any patterns or triggers that make you seek approval from others. By becoming aware of these patterns, you can start to detach from them and choose a more empowering response.

Practice self-validation: Instead of relying on external validation, learn to validate yourself. Acknowledge your accomplishments, celebrate your progress, and offer yourself kind and compassionate self-talk. Focus on your own internal compass and trust your own judgment rather than seeking constant reassurance from others.

Seek genuine connections: Shift your focus from seeking validation to building genuine connections with others. Nurture relationships based on mutual respect, trust, and understanding. Surround yourself with people who support and appreciate you for who you are, rather than those who constantly criticize or undermine you.

Cultivate mindfulness and self-care: Engage in mindfulness practices such as meditation, deep breathing exercises, or yoga to develop present-moment awareness and reduce reactive responses. Prioritize self-care activities that help you relax, rejuvenate, and reconnect with yourself.

Challenge limiting beliefs: Examine any limiting beliefs you may hold about yourself or the need for constant validation. Replace them with positive and empowering beliefs that support your self-worth and inner peace. Affirmations and positive self-talk can be helpful tools in this process.

Embrace personal growth: Focus on personal growth and self-improvement instead of seeking validation. Set goals that are meaningful to you and work towards them. Celebrate your progress and achievements along the way, knowing that you are growing and evolving as an individual.

Remember, cultivating inner peace is an ongoing process that requires patience and self-compassion. Be gentle with yourself as you release defensiveness and let go of the need for constant validation. With time and practice, you can develop a deeper sense of self-acceptance, inner peace, and a stronger foundation of self-worth that is not dependent on external factors.

Here are some additional steps to help you cultivate inner peace and release defensiveness by letting go of the need for constant validation and approval:

Practice self-compassion: Treat yourself with kindness, understanding, and forgiveness. Recognize that everyone makes mistakes and experiences ups and downs in life. Instead of being overly critical or judgmental towards yourself, offer yourself the same compassion you would extend to a friend.

Focus on your values: Identify your core values and live in alignment with them. When you prioritize your values and live authentically, you develop a stronger sense of self and inner peace. Base your actions and decisions on what feels true and meaningful to you, rather than seeking external validation.

Release comparison: Avoid comparing yourself to others, as it often leads to feelings of inadequacy and the need for validation. Remember that each person's journey is unique, and your worth is not diminished by someone else's achievements or successes. Embrace your own path and focus on your personal growth.

Let go of perfectionism: Accept that perfection is an unrealistic expectation and that making mistakes is a natural part of life. Allow yourself to be imperfect and learn from your experiences. Embracing imperfections can free you from the constant pressure of seeking approval and help you find peace within yourself.

Practice assertiveness: Cultivate assertiveness in expressing your needs, desires, and boundaries. By clearly communicating your thoughts and feelings, you empower yourself and reduce the need for others' validation. Assertiveness allows you to stand up for yourself while maintaining respect for others.

Seek inner validation: Develop a deeper connection with your inner self through introspection, self-reflection, and self-awareness practices. Connect with your intuition and trust your inner voice when making decisions. Relying on your own internal validation can provide a more stable and fulfilling sense of peace and self-worth.

Engage in self-care activities: Take time for activities that bring you joy, relaxation, and rejuvenation. Engaging in hobbies, spending time in nature, practicing self-care rituals, or pursuing creative outlets can help you reconnect with yourself and cultivate inner peace.

Practice gratitude: Cultivate a gratitude mindset by focusing on the positives in your life. Appreciate the things you have accomplished, the relationships you cherish, and the experiences that have shaped you. Gratitude can shift your perspective and reduce the need for external validation by fostering contentment and inner fulfillment.

Surround yourself with positivity: Surround yourself with positive influences, whether it's uplifting books, supportive friends, inspiring mentors, or motivational resources. Surrounding yourself with positivity can strengthen your inner resilience and provide encouragement on your journey to cultivating inner peace.

Seek professional support if needed: If you find that releasing defensiveness and letting go of constant validation is challenging, consider seeking support from a therapist or counselor. They can provide guidance, tools, and a safe space to explore underlying issues and develop strategies to cultivate inner peace.

Remember that cultivating inner peace is a personal journey, and it may take time to fully release defensiveness and let go of the need for validation. Be patient and compassionate with yourself as you navigate this process, and celebrate the progress you make along the way.

Chapter 9

Embracing Imperfection - Embodying Authenticity

Embracing imperfection and embodying authenticity is a powerful journey of self-discovery and personal growth. It involves letting go of the unrealistic pursuit of perfection and instead embracing the beauty of your true self. Here are some key aspects to consider when seeking to embrace imperfection and embody authenticity:

Releasing the need for perfection: Perfectionism can be a relentless pursuit that brings unnecessary stress and self-criticism. Recognize that perfection is an unattainable ideal and that true beauty lies in embracing your flaws and quirks. Shift your focus from seeking perfection to striving for personal growth and self-improvement.

Embracing mistakes as valuable learning experiences: Mistakes are an inevitable part of life, and rather than viewing them as failures, see them as opportunities for growth. Each mistake provides a chance to learn, develop resilience, and gain wisdom. Embrace the lessons learned from your errors and let them guide you towards personal and professional growth.

Cultivating self-acceptance: Acceptance of oneself is fundamental to embracing imperfection. Recognize that you are unique and that your individuality is what makes you special. Focus on your strengths, values, and passions, and appreciate the journey of self-discovery that you are on. Celebrate the progress you make rather than dwelling on perceived shortcomings.

Celebrating your unique qualities: Embodying authenticity means honoring and celebrating your unique qualities, including your strengths, talents, and even your vulnerabilities. Embrace your authentic voice, thoughts, and emotions. Avoid comparing yourself to others and instead acknowledge and appreciate your own journey and experiences.

Practicing self-compassion: Be kind to yourself during this process. Treat yourself with the same love, compassion, and understanding that you would offer a close friend. Acknowledge that you are human and that it's okay to make mistakes and have imperfections. Practice self-care, nurture your well-being, and prioritize activities that bring you joy and fulfillment.

Embracing imperfection and embodying authenticity is an ongoing process. It requires self-reflection, self-awareness, and a commitment to personal growth. By letting go of the need for perfection and embracing your authentic self, you can cultivate a greater sense of self-acceptance, fulfillment, and genuine connection with others.

Here are a few more points to consider when embracing imperfection and embodying authenticity:

Embracing vulnerability: Authenticity often requires being vulnerable and open. Allow yourself to be seen and heard as your true self, even if it means showing your imperfections or expressing your emotions. Vulnerability can deepen connections with others and create more meaningful relationships.

Letting go of external expectations: Society, culture, and the media often impose unrealistic standards of perfection. Recognize that these external expectations are often unattainable and not a true reflection of who you are. Focus on aligning with your own values, desires, and aspirations, rather than trying to meet the expectations of others.

Honoring your intuition: Your intuition is a powerful guide when it comes to embracing authenticity. Listen to your inner voice and trust your instincts. Pay attention to what truly resonates with you and what feels right, even if it goes against societal norms or the opinions of others.

Surrounding yourself with supportive people: Surround yourself with individuals who accept and appreciate you for who you are. Seek out relationships and communities that encourage authenticity, growth, and self-acceptance. Surrounding yourself with supportive people can provide a safe space for you to embrace imperfection and be your authentic self.

Practicing mindfulness: Mindfulness can help you become more present and accepting of the present moment, including your imperfections. Practice observing your thoughts and emotions without judgment or attachment. Cultivate self-awareness and self-compassion through mindfulness practices such as meditation or journaling.

Embracing flexibility and adaptability: Embracing imperfection means being flexible and adaptable in the face of challenges or unexpected outcomes. Embrace the idea that life is a constant journey of growth and change. Learn to pivot, adjust your expectations, and find beauty in the unpredictability of life.

Remember, the journey of embracing imperfection and embodying authenticity is unique to each individual. It's a personal exploration and discovery of what truly matters to you and what makes you feel alive. Be patient with yourself, celebrate small victories, and embrace the process with an open heart and mind.

Chapter 10

The transformative power of forgiveness in releasing defensiveness

Forgiveness is a deeply transformative and healing process that allows individuals to release defensiveness and move forward in their lives. It is an act of letting go of anger, resentment, and the desire for revenge towards someone who has caused harm or hurt. By embracing forgiveness, individuals can experience profound personal growth and find freedom from the emotional burdens that weigh them down.

One of the key aspects of forgiveness is its ability to break the cycle of defensiveness. When we hold onto grudges or harbor resentment, we build walls of protection around ourselves. These walls manifest as defensiveness, which can prevent us from fully engaging with others and experiencing genuine connections. By forgiving, we choose to dismantle these walls, opening ourselves up to vulnerability and authentic relationships.

Forgiveness also frees us from the negative emotions that come with holding onto past grievances. When we carry anger and resentment, it consumes our energy and affects our overall well-being. It can lead to chronic stress, anxiety, and even physical health problems. By forgiving, we release these toxic emotions and create space for healing and personal growth. Forgiveness allows us to reclaim our inner peace and regain control over our emotions.

Moreover, forgiveness offers an opportunity for personal transformation and growth. Through the act of forgiving, we develop empathy, compassion, and understanding. It requires us to put ourselves in the shoes of the person who has hurt us and see their humanity beyond their actions. In doing so, we cultivate a broader perspective and learn to see beyond our own pain.

Forgiveness is not about condoning or excusing harmful behavior. It does not mean forgetting what has happened or pretending that the pain did not exist. Rather, it is a conscious choice to acknowledge the hurt and actively choose to release its grip on our lives. Forgiveness is a gift we give ourselves, as it allows us to break free from the chains of the past and create a brighter future.

Moving forward after forgiveness is a process that involves rebuilding trust, setting healthy boundaries, and engaging in self-care. It may take time to fully heal from the wounds inflicted, but forgiveness sets the stage for growth and renewal. It allows us to let go of the role of victim and reclaim our personal power.

In conclusion, forgiveness holds immense power in releasing defensiveness and promoting healing. It liberates us from the burden of resentment, cultivates empathy and understanding, and paves the way for personal growth. By embracing forgiveness, we can move forward with grace and compassion, fostering healthy relationships and a more peaceful inner world.

Here are some additional points about the power of forgiveness:

Enhanced Emotional Well-being: Forgiveness has a profound impact on our emotional well-being. By letting go of negative emotions associated with past hurts, we experience a sense of emotional liberation. This can lead to reduced stress, improved mood, and increased overall happiness.

Improved Relationships: Forgiveness plays a crucial role in repairing and strengthening relationships. When we forgive others, we create space for reconciliation and restoration. It allows for the possibility of rebuilding trust, fostering deeper connections, and resolving conflicts in a healthier and more constructive manner.

Self-Healing: Forgiveness is not solely about the other person; it is also an act of self-healing. Holding onto resentment and anger can be emotionally exhausting and can hinder our personal growth. By forgiving, we prioritize our own well-being and focus on our own journey of healing and self-improvement.

Empowerment and Freedom: Choosing to forgive empowers us by giving us control over our own emotions and actions. It frees us from being stuck in a victim mentality and allows us to take charge of our lives. Forgiveness enables us to break free from the chains of the past and create a future that is not defined by our past hurts.

Spiritual Growth: Forgiveness is often considered a spiritual practice that promotes growth and enlightenment. Many spiritual traditions emphasize forgiveness as a pathway to inner peace and spiritual awakening. It enables us to cultivate qualities such as compassion, humility, and acceptance, leading to a deeper connection with ourselves and others.

Positive Ripple Effects: The power of forgiveness extends beyond ourselves and can have a positive impact on the world around us. When we forgive, we create a ripple effect of compassion and understanding. It inspires others to adopt forgiveness as well, contributing to a more forgiving and empathetic society.

Inner Strength and Resilience: Forgiveness requires immense strength and courage. It is a testament to our resilience and ability to rise above pain and adversity. By practicing forgiveness, we develop a greater sense of inner strength and resilience, which helps us navigate future challenges with grace and composure.

Remember that forgiveness is a personal journey, and it may not happen overnight. It requires patience, self-reflection, and a willingness to let go. While it can be challenging, the transformative power of forgiveness is immeasurable, offering us the opportunity to heal wounds, release defensiveness, and embrace a life of peace and growth.